An
Overdose
of Meditation

IRENE
MITCHELL

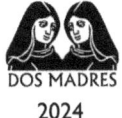

DOS MADRES
2024

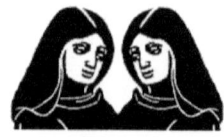

DOS MADRES PRESS INC.

P.O. Box 294, Loveland, Ohio 45140

www.dosmadres.com   editor@dosmadres.com

Dos Madres is dedicated to the belief that the small press is essential to the vitality of contemporary literature as a carrier of the new voice, as well as the older, sometimes forgotten voices of the past. And in an ever more virtual world, to the creation of fine books pleasing to the eye and hand.

Dos Madres is named in honor of Vera Murphy and Libbie Hughes, the "Dos Madres" whose contributions have made this press possible.

Dos Madres Press, Inc. is an Ohio Not For Profit Corporation and a 501 (c) (3) qualified public charity. Contributions are tax deductible.

Executive Editor: Robert J. Murphy

Illustration & Book Design: Elizabeth H. Murphy
www.illusionstudios.net

Typeset in Adobe Garamond Pro & SF New Republic
ISBN 978-1-962847-13-1
Library of Congress Control Number: 2024941950

ACKNOWLEDGEMENTS

Grateful acknowledgement is made to the editors of the following publications in which these poems first appeared:

The Deronda Review: "Enter the World," "A Change in theWeather"

Stone Poetry Journal: " Stars to Earth: Over"

Waterways: Poetry in the Mainstream: "The Relative Glory of Battle" (under the title "She Prunes Her Redbuds")

UCity Review: "Standard Deviation,"   "And Stands in for a Torrent of Ampersands," "July Fourth Honeypot," "Advice from Jonas Berry," "Harvest," "Taking Care of Business," A Hearty Repast," "Vapors Tossed," "In Attendance," "Connecting Rays," "Inner Fruit," "Vanitas"

Eunoia Review: "Perfect"

Open Doors Review (Florence, Italy): "Direct Action and Useful Knowledge"

For their contribution toward the making of this book, copious thanks go to:

Daniela Bertol, research artist, for the cover image *Body + Space* from her series *Geometries of Living.* Used by permission of the artist.

Liba Cacalova, Czech poet, for the author photo.

Mark Hirschberg, my husband, for flirting with all the poems.

Tamara Gaskell, Director of the Roeliff Jansen Library Branch, for hosting my poetry readings as part of the "Poetry in the Branches" program.

For my family

The truths of the earth continually wait;
they are not so conceal'd either.

Walt Whitman,
Carol of Words, from *Leaves of Grass*

Table of Contents

THE SUBLIMINAL THOUGHT FACTOR

SOMETHING ELSE, PLEASE?

Memories Come Knocking

COME IN

Thoughts followed by afterthoughts
followed by memories
frame this composition,

a confetti
of chords and cadences.

I would not mind your help
with the instrumentation, especially
the interpretation.

As you may have guessed, I am searching
for the rhythm of *more*
in which rhythm becomes rendition.

My ambition is to make the score brief
and hot with a tendency to mesmerize.

Thanks in advance for your suggestion.
I trust you, and enlist you.

May the music be cosmic and natural.
Taste and see.

Then having sampled,
allow the reverberations to reveal
what you, at your core,
see as useful to the process.

Lean back at your leisure
in a modern chair
and listen for any charms, spells,
broodings, or incantations —
all of equal value.

VINES, LEAVES, AND BRANCHES

What will be the song of the day?
A rhapsody called Enlightenment?
A symphony entitled Enchantment?
Entirely dependent on the weather —
yes, that fickle.

The vines have gone, uninvited, beyond
the tops of trees.
That is today's rub.

Why look for certainties, after all,
and their inherent dullness.
Give latitude to fictive strains because vines
have branches.
Anything is then possible through imagination.

First the withering
of the hardy leaves, then their downward
fall, all to be restored
after a few months on freeze.
That is a rhythm I can understand
for it is sensible and overall romantic
if you can stick around for the show.

Among the invited are many poets.
Imagine them all on the branches of a tree.
Who has not wanted to be a poet on a branch?
That is a delicate prospect
considering the multitude of poets and branches
wanting to sway in the breeze.

FORMULAS THAT MAKE A LIFE A LIFE

It is true that I do not remember
how the yellow plate from Royal Stafford
in Burslem, England (*The Heart of the Potteries)* broke.
There were originally five yellow plates, now three
so that makes it twice that I do not recall
the breakage.

I caught on to every other fleeting occurrence
of the past twenty-four hours,
proving there is plenty of oxygen left. However,
that announcement is predicated on the idea
that there is only so much oxygen
to be had per person,
proving that I can calculate sets of chinaware with the best
of the potters and plotters
though it is impossible to fathom the tables, charts
and formulas that make a life a life
for that depends upon where (the sun
is next intruding), or how (memory ignites),
or when (the horizon returns to one heedless gray),
or who (is asking), or why.

How did I gravitate to this post, all observant
and no motivation?
Yet it is a way perfectly designed
for my sort.

CLOSING TIME

I hesitate to reminisce,
fearing faulty interpretation.
Like a crowd of starlings in the square
there are just too many memories to monitor.

I draw the line in favor of ease.
As soon as I begin to ponder a point,
I wait until the moment passes
and fill it with an inspiring detail
such as how well read was Carlos Fuentes.

To honor detachment is my smug design,
my way of keeping secure the beauty
of the day which, by its end reveals
there may have been possibilities
to uncover which I chanced not to see.
The final moments of midnight
entice, for it is at this closing time that passions
seem truer and beauty more obvious.

Then follows the entry into morning,
signaling unease
for it is at this open time that memories come knocking.

STANDARD DEVIATION

Resting after a fall never means
not getting up at all, but resting just until
worries begin their flight.

And for that relief, all that is needed
is a down pillow, and high windows to deliver
a share of moon's ambient light.
Or is this break a dumbness
and excuse,
another silly respite
just to put vexations right?

With no more to lose, it is time now to fracture
useless worry.

This resolve places me handily
on the brink of happiness,
just at the door of delight,
neatly positioned at the edge of comfort.

AND STANDS IN
FOR A TORRENT OF AMPERSANDS

And how proceed?
Through wind *and* rain, by luck
and prowess until the edges frame
a mere garden patch
and any weeds are devil's work *and* hell
to hoe *and* the winning weed has resisted
any wilting.

And how advance through this garden
while building core *and* muscle
and, at the same time, empathy?

And will the happy gardener,
having reaped *and* sown *and* hoed alike,
live *and* thrive?

A ROUGH NIGHT

The remaining fault-line now
is the waistline. Otherwise, the decades
have been kind and muscle-tone is tight,
out there with the best.

It is sheer memory that is most
troublesome. It does not come when called.
Treachery!

It is all right to name
names, those involved in this treachery,
those foes of light, those mistrusters
of imagination, those miscreants of the written word.

It is all right to name names, and to reference
a proper practitioner of words
such as the professor of metaphysics.
How do I know I exist? asked the student.
And *who* is asking?

All right, let the past unfold and the words with them.
It is no one's past but mine
and includes one rough night too many.

Through the morning haze which shields the deer
hunters are firing warning shots
wounding my skittish ear.
After enduring several volleys
that aim for the heart, I fall hard
for love of dawning day, calling birds,
earthbound sunlight.

FALLING

We leave nothing
to chance
because we are well-mannered.
When we march through the dead leaves
with respectful reserve,
it is their end we are celebrating,
not our own.
Leaves are now drifting to the ground
where they land safely
which is more than we can say for some
astronauts

Likewise, it is our duty to watch
the stars to be sure they really twinkle
but they do seem happy up there, so effervescent.
Although we are beginning to tread on them
we will never put out their lights
as we have done time and time again
with other brightnesses.

Through yellow and scarlet leaves we wander,
never kicking or stomping
because we are well-mannered.
After all, it is the leaves' endgame we are celebrating
not our own wounds or mortality.

It has been suggested
that we think a little more about our own demise
and delve into that darkness as protection

now that the air is so cool and the sunny day
is in high glory. As for other things falling,
there is still plenty to worry about.
What is under those piles of leaves?

MISADVENTURES OF A CROCODILE
IN TOXIC WATERS

Considering the various ills of the year,
including ill-said,
it is still possible to wonder
about a crock's fascination with pandemonium
when he surfaces in the morning, ill-prepared.

Every day there looms
an ill-wrought scheme perpetrated
by this ill-designed reptile,
the Reviled Crocodile of Intimidation.

We have seen his teeth many times
and sense him lurking in the swamp
where he is making a toxic mess of things.

He means trouble.
His sinister appetite may be agitated
at any time into a cold-hearted danger,
raw, impenetrable, pathetically repetitive,
all those favorite figments and neuroses
(the cultural counterpart of genes)
stuck in a region of his mind.
What a crock!

After all our years at school
it does not take realization by degree
to understand there is little comparable
to the first iteration of a troublesome thing.

A Change in the Weather

HEARD ON A WALK IN THE WOODS

Should happiness and wonder revert
to regret, undertake the usual remedy,
a walk in the woods to admire the trees.
There compose some lines in praise
of beauty and wandering.

Do not bother to invoke past follies,
in itself a folly,
but call these forays *Experience*
and take them as they come
year to year,
employing all the threads
that seem appropriate to the occasion
as this walk in the woods
even while witnessing the performance
of words spiraling in a continual air-lift
until all the bare thoughts, defiant
in their nakedness,
reveal
there is something fluttering in the elm—
a leaf or a bird.

A CHANGE IN THE WEATHER

The age of anxiety isn't an historical age,
but an individual one, an age to be repeated
constantly through history.
                    John Koethe, *The Age of Anxiety*

An eight-pound weight has been lifted,
restoring clarity.
Now to parse the day
according to its splendors and woes.
Is this truly the mercurial twenty-fourth year
of the millennium?

Still present am I, far-vision excellent except
for a flow of unwanted (damned) flashes
of light entering the camera;
still alert to undercurrents and wind currents;
still resolved to explore more.

Lately, though it is the world which may be mellowing,
it seems that I, too, am bending,
easing up on scrutiny and analysis
to focus on plain (but first-rate) ideas,
wanting to be all-inclusive toward the end.
May it be not a momentous end
but an ordinary one, like a sudden (silent) change
in the weather.

IN ATTENDANCE

All tickets are on the table
and a merry treat it will be,
the pressures of preparation
long forgotten.
That is how the day should flow,
with a *hey-nonny-no*
and a dance to go.

Attending the concert
means packing only a few reminders.
I wend my way to the arena
without error or self-judgment.
Yet there are in the bag explicit cautions
which trail each other as the clouds,
expansive and close,
a useful omen for the watchful soul.

To keep going in such a manner
means assuming a behavior
bold enough to stomp through fire
whether for mirth or misery I am uncertain.
Right now, a little ferocity would go a long way
because waiting outside the theatre is that hero-
loving
audience of which I am part.

My presence here is alive
with references and points.
I have recorded in my journal
(having used this weapon before)
all the ways to join the crowd
and wake replenished.

THE RELATIVE GLORY OF BATTLE

Dedicated as she was to collecting arachnids,
depositing more specimens in the jar
became a sticky wicket
similar to the conundrum occurring outside
her window and toward the hill
concerning the over-branching redbuds
which had been pining all summer
even as she formulated her plan
for their resuscitation.

Are there any outstanding curses
upon these redbuds? she wondered.

A cavalier with a sturdy steed and sharp rapier
came to her rescue, citing too many spiders and snakes.
They have slumbered long enough, she determined.
What is your fee for pruning?

His fee was as high as the treetops
so she undertook the rescue mission herself,
reveling in the glory of battle.

By high noon the sun's red radiance
photo-sensitized the hills
and the redbuds renewed their promise
to shelter robins and butterflies
for her continued observance.

Shortly thereafter,

an error was made concerning
the element of air
which rushed by as a pruning wind
dismembering some limbs and disparate branches,
bequeathing to her an acre's rendition of nudity.

As for the remaining trees,
there was not a snide remark among them.

THE TROUBLE WITH THE BEDROCK

A person is like a mountain;
highs, lows. presence, longevity.
There may be splendors, too.

In fact, there is generally little conflict
within the mountain range
or in the valley.
Every hour instructs and when we learn
we are happy and not likely to fail.
That is a restful notion.

Speaking of rest,
for lack of vigor
I have suspended my search
for the complex intrigue

Something is taking shape during this sunny
respite on a deck of Brazilian mahogany.
I will send an envoy to the field
to discover what it is.

There is a high probability it is a new dirge
which the bedrock of familiar troubles
(also known as early memories)
cannot erode.

An early memory is of a bird
like a girl
atop her father's shoulders
at the lion's cage. *Hold tight*, he says.
That lion hasn't eaten since yesterday.

To one contemplating longevity,
that is sacred advice.

CONNECTING RAYS

If agile enough to negotiate a slope
it is recommended
to escalate to a hill, even if that hope
resembles Hilton's lost horizon. At least
there is sky involved and no sign
of a crater below. Therefore
no need of ladders, weaponry,
or papal prayers, for sky
has as much to do with rain as with prayer
and that argues for fair days ahead,

ensuring that the Perseids
will shower, as usual, on August 11
in the Western Hemisphere
and the connecting rays
of patience and equilibrium might prevail
over slope, hill and horizon.

A SOLO EXERCISE

Rain is not useful
for this soul's drought.
A downpour delivers
no relief
but when heat is applied
to the back of the neck
a more placid physicality is created.

Why this stiffness
where the cranium meets the neck?
It is borne of worry and worry never
accomplishes anything but a compounding
of anxious visions about the coming hours.

This is a solo expedition to eliminate
the discontent which poisons like cadmium.

Trying to reap the most lavish
and pleasant of visions is an exercise
which comes up short
when there is no next of savvy kin
with whom to celebrate.

Therefore, my indulgent audience,
I stand before you at this crucial age
when youth means everything to a face.

TAKING CARE OF BUSINESS

On the ochre path to the orchard
we meet some seekers of fruit.
We converse about our choices
and weigh which fruits are the most well-appointed,
considering how much more economical it would be
to let them ripen on the branch, thus giving them time
to engage with their fellow fruits about the rude hands
soon to pluck them,
disturbing their cool nights and charmed daylight
as they grow riper daily at the sun's pleasure.

By that we weigh and measure their fitness
and attend to ours.

Feeling sultry as the day is long,
warning each other not to overdue,
we go on gathering
because now we are old and need more fuel
since life has been unfolding in weary part and parcel
carried along by bits of bitumen to warm the stove
and keep the flame alive.

HOW CATARACTS, LIKE A CAT, INTERACT

> And hand in hand at the edge of the sand,
> they danced by the light of the moon.
> Edward Lear, *The Owl and the Pussy-cat*

Bearing in mind the few faults
the eyes are guilty of,
she renewed her partnership with them
while imploring the retina to transfix on the beautiful
and keep that image
for the longest possible hold.
Never had this directive been more vital
because the beautiful was increasingly
hard to find
and, once beheld, was ever more precious
because the old lens was becoming now
a waterfall.

As the eye surgeon tells it, diminishing light
renders one incapable
of seeing clearly through the falls
without the aid of a scalpel.

Thereafter, Aqueous, the owl and Vitreous, the cat
went to sea in a beautiful pea-green boat.
They took some honey and plenty of rummy
using both their humours to stay afloat.

On shore by moonlight
they measured their eyedrops
with a runcible spoon but the *all-clear*
was indistinct. Nowhere near.

CLARITY AND CONFIDENCE

The heart calls the soul
calls the starched white cotton to arms.
En garde!
Something is up.

Something the opposite
of a placid mooring.

The heart calls on clarity
(when confidence dissolves)
certain that it will not combust
for a light-year so that one may live
on its bright power, renewing
the strength of soul which was assured
in days of old.

Sun leans toward possible
so that the vision of a parasol
is fully conceived before long
and those private sessions of doubt
clear the way to a placid mooring,
establishing a power
which would be criminal to waste.

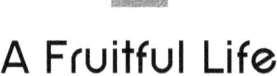

A Fruitful Life

HARVEST

To wish for more
than this sweet acre of fruit trees
is to wish in vain,
for here is found plenty of fig, peach and plum.
I am sorting the fruit (with the eye of a doe)
according to ripeness and color.

On the picnic table is a vessel
heaped with fortifying morsels. Nearby
is a cup of clarified juice.
The remaining pulp is labeled
Attention well-paid.

A preserve of sunlight pierces
the shade of the fruit trees.
Too much rainfall
has blackened the leaves.
The doe is speeding by in the rain.

A HEARTY REPAST

I abhor a list
for its dullness, its lack of insight,
arcane references.

What I have been saying all along
I will say again, although specifications
as to meaning are not yet firm.
Please get back to me
the day after next.
By then I will be able to reconsider operations.

As of now, I have swept the orchard clean
and started over, old husks buried,
grasses native to the watched soil
cleanly mown.

The field of operations is fertile with new thoughts
and persuasions.
Some lilies can read thoughts
but at this meal there are nasturtiums on the plate.
There are those who would not eat a flower,
feeling full already.

ADVICE FROM JONAS BERRY

When next we meet at the corner store
to buy a piece of fruit,
do not be shocked, for we might bring up
our nightmares, or more seasonally,
country airs if it is the year of the lyric
and it is usually that.

Therefore, say what you know
but what is that compared to each working opus
gathering strength in the world at this moment?
Now grab the scythe and trim all ordinary impressions
whether shining on the hill or loitering on your horizon.
Let ideas come and their versions, too, unstoppable.
Any thought worth thinking
is compost for the next eloquent outpouring.

I tell you this so you may save
yourself from having to re-tell it to your fellows
who have never comprehended it
before I told it to you. I hope it is not precious of me to say
that I have no idea when I will have these fruitful thoughts
again. As a warning, they may be surreal.

VANITAS

As for me, I find that certain kinds of misunderstanding are full of useful hints.

Saul Bellow, *Humbolt's Gift.*

It was a curious, unexpected happening,
a peculiarity which was becoming ever more curious
perhaps due to an original misunderstanding
about the circumstances, let us say, of my existence
and the elements that plague me including –or leading to–
oddities in blood pressure, about which I have had
numerous conversations with my heart.
They only led to more disruptive moods.

My canvas, if I could paint at all,
would depict my *Vanitas,* all the concrete elements
of this life which had meaning and were restorative
whether hinted at or in the form of such helpful assurances
as a needle, a spool of thread, a glove.
I imagined that once the needle was threaded
and the glove's worn fingers sewn before the fault line gave way,
the rest of the work would be done to capacity,
easily executed without contradiction or misunderstanding.

JULY FOURTH HONEYPOT

Mine was the sort of intelligence
that lazed on a carpet under the dome
in excellent weather
in order to free itself from the menace
of melancholy.

Such an indulgence
would often cause the carpet to float,
restoring to lightness all sweet delicacies
of the mind, and prophesying that a select bowl of fruit
and flowers
would be ready for the table
that sits upon the floating carpet.

The bowl of fruit is a private kaleidoscope
of sweetened meditations
taking place under an assemblage of scudding clouds.
In this bowl is also a honeypot,
a flower resembling a chalice.
It acts as divine inspiration for a fruit and flower competition.

After plenty of clamor, pomegranate wins honors
for seeds galore and for literature.
The runner-up is pearly everlasting, each white flower
resembling a tiny wedding bouquet.

Imagine a woman in her wedding dress
on the Fourth of July! She floats on a carpet
holding a honeypot. It is excellent weather.

The carpet's velvet nap is wearing
because it is real velvet and that is its course.

STARS TO PLANET EARTH: OVER

The moon went barreling by.
Next of kin, the combustible stars
(as recorded by satellite), felt honored,
while down here ancient stalagmites
caught some of that moonlight through cracks
in their rocky dens.

Back at the ranch we lazed
with a third mint julep, as though nothing in our world
was amiss. That is what we were diligently taught.
We filled another glass with more julep than mint
and reclined with some long-playing bluegrass.

There is other music yet to be conceived,
as indicated by birds on a wire
and fingers of fire on keys and strings.

The wonder is that there are ways
to preserve it all. All factoids can
be recorded and saved via balloon.
There are thousands of starry possibilities.

How did you come to amass such a list?
Man, I flirted with it and let it fly.

INNER FRUIT

Little do I know about the origins of calamity.
I did not travel far enough
for tears to fall

for on the route before me lay only the mystifying,
the fortifying,
the wry and the contradictory.

There were memories, too.

Now that I have the hang of it, more
memories come knocking,
not many burdens among them
or perhaps they were just being carefully handled
like a melon
so no bruising would occur
and the proud and perfect melon could then be served
alongside the cod caught, salted and stored.

Remembering, supposing, counting, assessing
is no way to spend the time. It is an overdose
of meditation.
Swim the endless pool, instead, to manage
breath. Indulge in floating.

Complete the crystallizing opus.
Why wait for tears to fall?

ENTER THE WORLD

Remove your personal self from the work
and enter the world like a continent.
Letters of Ted Hughes, to Olwyn Hughes

As a prelude to the actual entrance,
neither a skip nor a hop
will get one any closer.
A scramble, though it may provide
the needed element of rush,
will not be sufficient either.
To gain full entry into the world
as guardian of place and tribe,
crash and bang at the door
crying that there is so much more
to the sojourn, which is immanent.

Such a method is also reliable
if distance is what one is after, distance
being the dominant consideration
by which a thought is cast into the universe.

An extra heartbeat here, a word murmured there—
until the entry fee climbs.
Who among us has not felt a bolt of lightening
aimed right at the psyche
once it is understood that mortality has its limits
and age does its utmost to antagonize
one who has already entered the world,
one whose arrival was a rare jubilee,
one who interprets that life is more than an unrefined
spin with a trickle of substance.

Accompanied by the bold music
of trembling stars and charged auroras,
enter the searing glamor of the stratosphere.
Mind not to hurry the music along before the light changes
and a stranger world arrives in its contrary way.

VAPORS TOSSED

Meditations are vapors tossed
and upon their return
come messages
and provocations
sacred to the process.

As part of the innocence project
to protect against prejudice,
most meditations invite two worlds—
marvels of the mind unconfined
and those marvels which can be seen and heard
such as mourning doves minding their eggs.

Leaving them untouched means
these meditations can be archived,
preferably at the University of History and Inquiry
which holds every truth.

TASTE AND SEE

Not so deep
so as not to deceive,
the vessel fills.

The delicate contents, in this case
fruits on a bed of marigolds still
keeping a fragrance,
are eaten down to the last blossom,
relished as if pages in a manuscript.

Weighing whether to doubt or fidget
or claim the center
and there hold fast,
take a share of this bounty
for a fruitful life.

Search the actual, tangible pages,
hearing them murmur as you turn
from one to the other,
each page filling a hole in the foundation.

Gustate et videte.
Taste and see.

The Subliminal Thought Factor

THE ELUSIVE ART OF POSSIBILITY

You were right, Doris. The grass is singing.
Solace of an open space,
surety of the blank page in the open space
and what I was after was the sight of a damselfly,
the great cascade damsel breeding in grass
at the waterfall. She was roaring-fire red
and said to me in a voice both comfortable
and fake, *If anything should happen
I'm over here.*

This report is dictated by curiosity alone.
Why should I burn with envy
and consume every passion in this pursuit,
pretending to be just another
roaring-fire red damselfly.
My camouflage will be detected
leaving me to come and go as myself
until summer dies
and garlands in the room begin to weep.

You were right, Doris. Concentrate on the song
of the waterfall
while keeping a curious eye on the open space.

EXCELLENT GLIDER

I have only to read John Koethe
to glean how a moment glides
toward the next unalterable moment,
carrying with it unease or unknowing,
sometimes pleasure
because at this late stage in the journey
to the pinnacle,
the many profound questions which still gather
deep in the heart's core
need to be further illuminated.
Laying my sword on the table, I review
these questions to calm the turmoil
now ripping by, the momentary rush of wind,
then the gliding.

LET'S SEE WHAT HAPPENS

When the music amplifies
will the sleeper mind?
It is time to dress, anyway, warmly
if possible, against the wind
and co-incidentally prepared if rain falls.

Let's see what happens.
If experience is real, may it last long
and be recorded
while aquifers of the mind
aspire to new propositions.

The Office of Resilience
presents many safe-as-you-go
propositions
to keep the aquifers in fresh supply
so as not to overburden the earth,
the music, the sleep, the sea.

Ocean liners have docked and are secured
in their space, loaded and bound now
for Newfoundland. Attention!
There is a high magnitude earthquake there.
Or is it a high category hurricane?
Let's see what happens.

THE MARKETPLACE

I have embraced
the mutual destruction
of tension and exclusion.

Out of that murder grows a new insight,
evermore enticing.
The details of its richness
have yet to unfold
for a sacrifice is involved.
It means changing the lingo
to a basic commodity for sale in the open
market of common thought.

As long as the neck is able to support
the cerebellum, I take the bait
and gather all the common thoughts
that muster
when I am not seeking.

CHECK THOSE METAPHORS!

How many tugs
equal a tear in the fabric?

There are not that many barriers to cross
but when a tear becomes a hole,
its repair with a fine needle
may be the avenging factor since the hole
was created by an intelligence with intent to corrupt.

Blame the silkworm or the moth
for they are ravenous.
One may mitigate
the actual damage
by examining the cloth.

We were told by the tailor to tread lightly here
because too many choices
can be as wearying
as too many metaphors,
except to metaphor-adorers.

THE WINGED ARCHIVES

Whether to simplify or amplify.
That is the question.
Whether to persist or retreat.

Damn these philosophical questions!
Full speed ahead!

There may be breakage along the way
and new questions arising
proving that the lifting and hauling
are what make a life
a life.

This life frames
the daily requisite, *I want, I need.*
Consult the archives
as to whether or not fulfilled.

There are pre-requisites, also
but those have been slain,
slain while music played in the anteroom
also known as the parlor.

From the parlor windows, the field can be seen
and all the details therein.
Questions will be arriving at a later date
as to how and whether
to proceed as conceived.

MIND-BODY EXERCISE

Excelsior – always upward

It does not hurt to lie down to exercise
the mind.
Millions of minds have done so
and enthusiastically wakened
(Excelsior!)
with no additional burdens
although it is necessary to keep at least a few
remaining burdens in tow
so they may be reinvented on a new page.

A new page records the details:
once he completed all the labors,
she was won
and off to the castle they rode,
a fine mind-body exercise of consequence,
good muscle-tone now achieved
and certain aspects of the mind improved.

Excelsior! they cried to the river
for it was lethargic.
The river, upon awakening, joyously
began to flow two ways, upward
and inward
carrying with it a distant sense of enlightenment.

A CONTRACT WITH FOLLY

The last leaf to fall shredded my resolve
so that I considered resolving anew.
To do this, I was locked into imagining
a future filled with practicalities
rather than with the follies with which I had always
maintained a contract.

I will record the following folly:

One of my parents is a bird,
the other an elm. When something
flutters in the elm, it is the other.
I watch them until they break
toward the next dawn
or until the last leaf falls.

I heard the leaf
tumble without a gripe
and heard the bird weeping
and calling.

MOOD AND CONSEQUENCE

I regard with interest
a contrast before unnoticed—
Yes, that moment was a lucky one, this one not so lucky.

It is all fat for the pages,
indulgence for the oncoming days,

still fresh in mind
the ground I mistook for fertile.

Nor would going deeper
reveal much except that I kept affairs in order
for the record

and for the record
resisted regret.

ASCENDING

When prayers stack up,
their original premise not quite ready
for the voyage home,
the idea of prayer
remains latent in the mind's sphere.
This pattern provides comfort,
a flat plain to visit to prolong prayer
without lamentation
as if the plain were eternally fertile, invasive
outcroppings displaced by the wind.

It may seem like paltry sustenance
to outsiders,
but these very undertakings, also known as
underpinnings, lead to that significant prayer
called poetry.
I wave the wand to conjure even more
excited states of agitation.
These are usually forthcoming from on high.

The moon went west toward the Rockies,
its light on the crags.
Had I followed it, I would have cried
for its parting from the east
and prayed for its return to calmer waters,
prayed
in a sing-song language
of casava, papaya and bits of sugar cane
which restoreth the whole.

EQUAL DAY AND NIGHT

This thread explores
what day and night convey
beyond the sweet repair of sun and star.

Under August sun I lie with sea-foam lovers,
our charmed
voices casting fresh murmurings out to sea.

I explore scintillations
with watchers of the dark sky, searching
for an excellent society,
one which remembers itself in the stars,
a centuries old nether-numerology
with evolving definitions

Day and night convene
as predictably as the flight of birds.

Sparrows call from branch to branch,
tree to tree.
Thoughts followed by afterthoughts
wing ahead, easily.

Something Else, Please?

ENTER, EXIT: A CO-EVOLUTION

Who are we but mere commoners,
commoners with variations
on a language,
language which includes elements
of loneliness,
lonely because fast-disappearing beauty
is no longer the company
it once was, fast-disappearing
along with other comforts
though there are those who continue to pursue those comforts,
pursue them even through damaging winds.

I tell you this because in the long days and nights
during which we are losing muscle, loads
still need to be borne,
borne because the sky is imperishable
and offers rewards.
Better to stay and plough,
plough through the altered earth, honoring
all common passersby,
though the naked eye proves
less discerning than it once was.

It is quiet now.
We are awash in a new ecoregion
in which only hunter-gatherers, harvesting edible
bird's nests and wild honey, thrive.
Ours is a co-evolution of language and genes.
Clothes are fashioned from tree-bark.

Rolled-up leaves carry messages from one
commoner
to another
throughout the endangered forest.

SOMETHING ELSE, PLEASE?

Every day is graduation day
proving that there is always something else.
At Key West, for example,
the sun goes down like a parachute.
A little renegade is running toward
his mother's camera
in a white cotton Easter suit,
angelic to the eye. We expect him
to graduate by and by.

How fine it is to polish the details.
In the story-telling arena there is no room
for posturing. All data must be refined
and approved before earning admittance
to the lexicon of fresh impressions.

Still fresh in the mind are pre-graduation
academic notions
which must find a place, for surely
they are valuable and not to be squandered
in a noisy, evolving fiction
but forwarded to something else, something unforgettable.

The surf at Bahia Honda, for example,
is warm and wild
and much may be made of its waves graduating
to a swimmable delicacy of advancing words,
an orchestration of three chords and a truth.

Something else, please?

PERFECT

That day, the river was serene.
I walked the edge,
then faster for the happiness of the hour
as I was limber and full of soul,
all-aware,
one with air and sun.

Searching for a fair spot
to fish for perch, I remembered
that what bites today
depends on the bait,
assuming that an empty line means
fish have fought for it.

Something else will have to take the place
of the lure.

Call it love this time,
and may it endure,
drawn from the deep.

While the ardor is fresh, I might add a wash
for mystery
and call it one perfect day
on the way to another.

STRIFE OVER TRIFLES

Clamshell gray, beak yellow.
Hard to tell this gull from that
for the shoreline is foreign in fog,
an indistinct scene of orts and fragments.

I intrude upon a piping plover and go my way
thinking how little I know about birds
and less about love
except for a teasing glitter, a vague priority
like a plover's plaintive note
which insinuates something else.

Why such strife over trifles?
That is the very thing
I would love to know,
but don't.

A FINER FABRIC THAN FEAR

Why this rush to explore?
There is still time to gather and preserve
the spoils of previous explorations,
building details of the original tripe
to monumental significance
if anyone is interested.

The mission
is to find rooms, countries,
whole kingdoms in which fear
plays no part.

Yet fear is confessed in the retelling
if anyone is listening
because confession is the enricher of souls.
To confess fear is to free the thread
from the bobbin
so that the tailor beholds
a now exquisite embroidery.

The embroidery shows a convex solid,
an icosahedron having twenty
triangular sides which convey a meaning:
trust in the wisdom of the universe.

DIRECT ACTION AND USEFUL KNOWLEDGE

This is the year
of our knowledge
about the strange planetary fog
which the telescope could not penetrate
because the fog reached the stratosphere.

This is also the year of our confusion
about whether or not to study that fog
toward an honorary degree in letters
which might only lead to a position at the post office.

Direct action is more useful,
the better to fight forest fires
where they are burning
and save the deer and partridges.

I have shopped at Selfridge's
but that store is no longer there
and Coin Firenze is in a different location.
This is useful knowledge.

As knowledge, it clears the density
and leads to a delicious diversity,
a Pitti Immagine of color and fashion,
a hit-parade of clarity and confusion.

INTO THE MOUTH OF THE WOLF

Humble yet thriving in its way
like a houseplant which has given so many years
of pleasure,
the enriched soil of a home plantation
enhances an exploratory space wherein
days grow greener.

The ice cream wagon still rolls
down the concrete streets,
its jingle calling a rhyme remaining
in the air long after that repair
to the country
where children thrive while tending
their garden mounds
and stores of curious houseplants.

They all grow sturdy,
making their way toward the sun
and don't forget the stars
shining in syncopation, so far, through those happy days.

LINGERING THOUGHTS ABOUT LASTING LOVE

We are not used to seeing each other
unadorned
in soul and body (as is our custom)
until the vows are taken
and we are infinitely surprised
by all that beauty
which, in the bath, cannot be resisted
but only polished
by the agonies of love. In the face
of this we blush and look pale
both at the same instant in which our souls meet.

That moment holds captive
a boundless region of emerald nights wrapped
in the gold of the zodiac.

LIFTED

Wanting to attain peerage
in the ranks, like a bird puffing up
against the cold, a little balloon
of insulating air, I cried to the breeze
Lift me
so that I now belong.

I strode from room to room
thinking it over, now here, now
there and over the field to Grandma's
house for some serious
philosophical conversation.

Grandma was planting
seeds next to the berry bush
and confided to me the sustaining
power of that exercise.
That is all you shall have of structure
today, she said as she carried a plant
to the kitchen window to show me
how well-behaved it was.
Hers was a nice kitchen, but it was not
my kitchen.

Coming up for air between the intervals,
I discovered that something in the realm
of clear thinking, was amiss.
I spied on my own kitchen windowsill
a begonia drawn to the light

for survival.
Its soft petals favored me, lifted and loved me
so that I floated toward the sky,
a little balloon of insulating air.

NOTES UPON REVIEWING THE PHOTOGRAPHS

Upon reviewing the photographs
I can let it be known
that their crumbling presence
continues to draw me
toward, as they say in the lower reaches,
an orgasmic question, a central probe:
where and how did these vestiges
thrive
and what have they bequeathed to me
that I cannot live without?

My predicament is that I can hardly recall
through the photographs
the life on East Tenth Street,
the library, the barber shop's revolving pole,
the candy store for more joy
because *Almond Joy has nuts, Mounds don't,*
and other phenomena including more and more
female drivers, Carl Sandburg visiting the library,
ballet lessons for fifty cents
at the settlement house
(an errant baseball to the eye on the way),
torch songs via radio, and melancholy bluegrass
plaintive enough
to elicit tears.

What is the use of any crochet of memories
except to bind together early patterns
later to be deciphered as the life

of the mind.
One more poem entire.
Now a future can be seen,
intake and out, ready for exposure.

COSMIC LAW

With birds-eye clarity I see that the sky
is the same blue
as always with an occasional pink cloud.

Copying its easy flight plan
I fall into some reading, some writing,
some scowling at the cat,
some navigation of thoughts, and standard sky-watching.

When a band of clouds appears as boldly
as a chorus of afterthoughts, pressures
of the blood increase
and blood, like a bird, wants to go its own way,
coursing as it pleases, raising hell
if it desires.

Taking the meditative
course through airspace to guide altitude
and destination
means acknowledging the space-time continuum
and launching echoes from there

where the orchestrating pilot can keep a steady eye
on a view still green
and loveable.

ABOUT THE AUTHOR

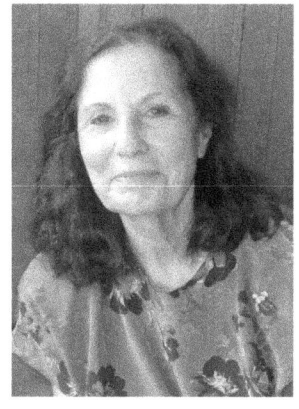

IRENE MITCHELL is the author of eight previous poetry collections, most recently *My Report from the Uwharries* (Dos Madres Press, 2022). Her *Selected Poems*, was published by FutureCycle Press in 2021. Dos Madres Press has published two other recent collections, *Clerestory* (2020), and *Fever* (2019). Mitchell taught Writing, English, and English to Speakers of Other Languages in inner city and rural New York. There she conducted poetry workshops and served as judge in poetry competitions. Formerly poetry editor of Hudson River Art Magazine, Mitchell is known for her collaborations with visual artists and composers. Her poems were set to music for piano and voice in an art-song cycle entitled *Past All Doors,* which debuted in Stuyvesant, New York. Several of her poems have been executed as broadsides and exhibited *ad hoc* at local galleries and libraries. Mitchell's early correspondence with poetry editors and scholars is included in the final year's collection of The Aylesford Mss., archived at Indiana University's Lilly Library. Mitchell was a recent Associate Artist in Residence with Cornelius Eady at the Atlantic Center for the Arts.

.

www.ingramcontent.com/pod-product-compliance
Lightning Source LLC
Chambersburg PA
CBHW051546120626
46551CB00013B/1388